Families

Brothers and Sisters

Rebecca Rissman

www.raintreepublishers.co.uk
Visit our website to find out
more information about
Raintree books.

To order:

☎ Phone 0845 6044371

▤ Fax +44 (0) 1865 312263

✉ Email myorders@raintreepublishers.co.uk

Customers from outside the UK please telephone +44 1865 312262

Raintree is an imprint of Capstone Global Library Limited, a company incorporated in England and Wales having its registered office at 7 Pilgrim Street, London, EC4V 6LB – Registered company number: 6695582

Text © Capstone Global Library Limited 2011
First published in hardback in 2011
Paperback edition first published in 2012
The moral rights of the proprietor have been asserted.

Edited by Rebecca Rissman, Dan Nunn, and Catherine Veitch
Designed by Ryan Frieson
Picture research by Tracy Cummins
Production by Victoria Fitzgerald
Originated by Capstone Global Library
Printed and bound in China by Leo Paper Products Ltd

ISBN 978 1 406 22145 9 (hardback)
14 13 12 11 10
10 9 8 7 6 5 4 3 2 1

ISBN 978 1 406 22153 4 (paperback)
15 14 13 12 11
10 9 8 7 6 5 4 3 2 1

British Library Cataloguing in Publication Data
Rissman, Rebecca.
Brothers and sisters. -- (Families)
306.8'75-dc22

Acknowledgements
We would like to thank the following for permission to reproduce photographs: Corbis pp. 5 (©Randy Faris), 10 (©Edith Held), 19 (©Image Source); Getty Images pp. 4 (arabianEye), 8 (Edgardo Contreras), 9 (Karen Moskowitz), 13 (DK Stock/Guillermo Hung), 15 (Ryuichi Sato), 17 (Yellow Dog Productions); istockphoto pp. 6 (©Shelly Perry), 7 (©Gary Sludden), 14 (©James Blinn), 20 (©John Prescott), 21 (©Kristian Sekulic), 22 (©Diane Labombarbe), 23 a (©John Prescott), 23 b (©Shelly Perry); Shutterstock pp. 11 (©Jaren Jai Wicklund), 12 (©tonobalaguerf), 16 (©Yuri Arcurs), 18 (©Christopher Futcher), 23 c (©Jaren Jai Wicklund).

Front cover photograph of a brother and sister holding paper figurines reproduced with permission of Getty Images (American Images Inc). Back cover photograph of a brother and sister reproduced with permission of istockphoto (© James Blinn).

We would like to thank Anne Pezalla, Diana Bentley, and Dee Reid for their invaluable help in the preparation of this book.

Every effort has been made to contact copyright holders of material reproduced in this book. Any omissions will be rectified in subsequent printings if notice is given to the publisher.

Contents

What is a family?

A family is a group of people who care for each other.

People in a family are called family members.

All families are different.

All families are special.

What are families like?

Some families are big.

Some families are small.

Brothers and sisters

brother

sister

In some families there are brothers and sisters.

Brothers and sisters are called siblings.

Girl siblings are called sisters.

Boy siblings are called brothers.

Some brothers and sisters look alike.

Some brothers and sisters
look different.

Some brothers and sisters live with their parents.

Some brothers and sisters live away from their parents.

Some brothers and sisters share the same parents.

Some brothers and sisters have different parents. They are step-brothers or step-sisters.

Some brothers and sisters are adopted. They have joined a

 new family.

Do you have brothers or sisters?

Family tree

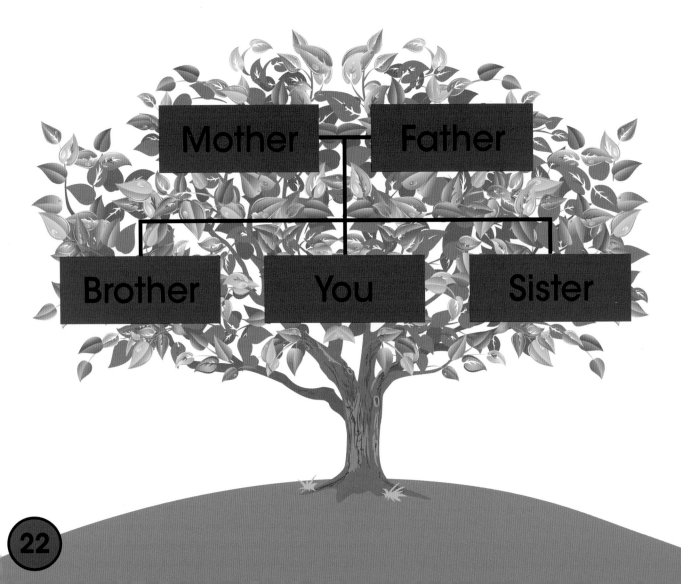

Picture glossary

 **adopted** invited into a new family. Many families adopt children.

 **member** person who belongs to a group

 **sibling** brother or sister

 **step-brother** or **step-sister** brother or sister with different parents

Index

Note to parents and teachers

Before reading

Explain to children that all families are different. Tell children that some families have only one child, while others have many children. Ask children to name their family members and list any brothers and sisters they might have.

After reading

- Explain to children that some families adopt children. This means that they welcome a new child into their family. Ask children if they know a family who has adopted a child.

- After reviewing the family tree on page 22, draw a family tree for one volunteer child on the board. Encourage children to go home and draw their own family trees.